FINISHING LINE PRESS

www.finishinglinepress.com

# The Late Hour

*poems by*

# Marjie Giffin

*Finishing Line Press*
Georgetown, Kentucky

# The Late Hour

## ACKNOWLEDGMENTS

"A Clear Wriggler" in *Synkroniciti*
"Brattle Street" in *So It Goes: The Journal of the Kurt Vonnegut Memorial
    Library, No. 6*
"Dead End" in the poet's chapbook, *Touring*
"Empty City" and "The Station at Kharkiv" in *Tipton Poetry Journal*
"Hondo, New Mexico" in *St. Katherine Review*
"Just a Bird" in *Agape Review*
"Mother Grim" in *Spirit and Place Anthology* and *Stormwash: Environmental
    Poems*
"October on the Shore" in *Of Rust and Glass*
"Place of Peace" in *Flying Island*
"The Late Hour" as a feature in *Heartland Society of Women Writers*
"The Plunge" in *Snapdragon: A Journal of Art and Healing*
"Touring" in *Northwest Indiana Literary Journal*

Publisher: Leah Huete de Maines
Editor: Christen Kincaid
Cover Art: Elisabeth Speckman
Author Photo: Elisabeth Speckman
Cover Design: Elizabeth Maines McCleavy

Order online: www.finishinglinepress.com
    also available on amazon.com

Author inquiries and mail orders:
Finishing Line Press
PO Box 1626
Georgetown, Kentucky 40324
USA

# Contents

*For Bailee, Emersyn, Parker,*
*Bronson, Tatum, and Luke*

# Invisible

is how I feel much of the time
now that I am an *older woman*
and of little use or importance
to the tempo of urban living,
the Captains of Industry
who keep the cogs rolling,
or youthful netizens who keep
the comments trolling. *Unseen*
is how I see myself even as I
eye the mirror and confirm
that I do exist. So I subsist
on meager rations of serious
communications and swallow
those words that the world
has no heart to hear. Yet I
have history to share,
choice nuggets of experience
that others might care
to learn. I suspect that I
am not alone, older women
encircling the globe, truth
on their lips muffled by
tastes catering to males
and the gloriously young.

## Lost Promise

More fetal in shape
than cocooned,
I am yet a pretzel
of late-aged
womanhood—
brittle when bent,
stiffened into myself
and not softly curled—
not likely to unfurl
with soaring wings
of wafting promise,
more likely to stay
still and spent.

## The Plunge

I am running out of time
but I'd like to slip down
the mossy steps
of my sister's pier
and plunge headfirst
without hesitation
into the still-chilled June waters
of her pristine Northern lake
and push off the stony bottom
and float and float and float—
perhaps as far as Canada—
where wild geese, arching,
would flap down at me
as I churned my aging body forward
and they would circle, nodding,
bestowing their respect.

## Contrast

I seek solitude to ease my mind—
sometimes just to sprawl on the lawn
and feel air whispering in my ears
and hear silence splaying around me.

I have stood under stars, alone,
breathing in and breathing out
and squinting at the nightscape
and discovering its cool balm.

No such calm can be found in crowds
on a beach or in passing masses
on city streets. Nor can soul searching
be reached in rooms of raucous music.

There's no peace to be had when
there's pushing and shoving and elbows
are touching. Quiet between us allows
each of our souls space to grow.

## The Late Hour

arrives early it seems and pits me
against the digital clock face
that dares me to defy its logic.
Defy it I must, for there are no hours
for my own doings and yearnings
unless I scavenge them from
the riff-raff moments of the end of day.

I am used to the scraps of life,
as a woman and more, a wife,
whose value cannot measure up
to the sexy perks of an executive
spouse—whose personal needs
get swallowed up by martini lunches
and after-hour cocktail soirees
and holiday parties *sans* wives.

Unholy work perhaps to labor long
by sinks and mounds of laundry
and then muster the zeal to steal
some time to pen a wistful line.
Yet fruitful work for sanity to be
saved and some remnants of self
to be salvaged in a day's late hour.

## When I Can't Cry

There are times
when I've tried to cry
and despite my need
for outlet and respite
not one single tear
has squeezed from my eye.

I've felt empty and dry
and though longing
for catharsis
I've been unable to muster
more than a sigh.

The spigot's not on
and though I do try
to cleanse and relieve
the heaviness inside
nothing seeps out—
I just cannot cry.

## Mine to Keep

The house is silent, and that's a blessing.
There is nothing less comforting than tumult
and noise. I pad around on slippered feet
and greet the quiet with a sense of peace.
I unplug the phone and pull the blinds.
Ready the quilt, warm the tea, choose
the book. Solitude has its own coy look.
I am my own companion, an easy one
to keep. The evening is mine—and deep.

## Just a Token

I once was hurt by an unforgivable act.
I didn't choose to forgive or to forget.

In the end, I did nothing to right the wrong.
I merely kept on keeping on.

To this day, I bear the scars.
The very memory of the injury mars

a relationship that was forever broken.
What's left is at best a substitute token

of what should have been something solid—
something now that's soiled and pallid.

## Just a Bird

*On the Surfside Condo Tragedy, Florida*

A baby bird falls into our chimney, and its plaintive
chirps disturb me as I lie upon the couch reading.

I know I cannot help the tiny thing, but as its cries
grow weaker and weaker, my heart begins to thrum.

My husband says *it's just a bird,* but my mind swirls
with visions of the condo collapse in Surfside.

A trapped bird, calling out with its last beat of life,
evokes images that I dare not let settle.

As I strain to hear and no more chirps resound,
I feel but an inkling of the despair of the loved ones

who gather and hope and pray and wait until word
reaches them that no more sounds can be heard.

## Brattle Street

I butt my head against a gust of biting wind
and let my crimson scarf whip across my face
and blind me to the ragged heap in front of me.

*What the hell?* I want to shout—*It's Harvard Square!*
as I dodge shapeless forms that dot the icy sidewalks,
humps and mounds slumped under faded wraps.

Nearby at The Charles, the lobby exudes warmth
as gushing alums crush one another, arms outstretched
and checkbooks open to embrace their alma mater.

Inside hallowed classrooms and well-endowed labs,
great minds from across the globe converge and converse,
tilting heads together to brainstorm and save the world.

On Brattle Street, students trudge through soot and slush,
intent in their pursuit of the higher arts and sciences,
resolved to right the wrongs and injustices that blight us.

Past fast food joints, coffee shops, bookstores, and pubs—
Harvard thinkers plod on and on, sidestepping the bodies
that so artlessly litter the landscape, block their progress.

I shake the snow from my scarf as I climb into a taxi—
take one last look as we pull from the curb. Some clumps
move, some stay still, and I have no diploma to explain it.

# Bereft

*On the Wildfire Destruction on Maui*

The Mauian man
face plastered flat against the screen
tears drooling around the lids
of his eyes
looks left and then right
as if gauging the breadth
of his world that's now
bereft

The interview is short
and clipped and breaks hearts
as the man summarizes his lot:
It's all gone
everything is gone
the scene behind him charred
and black and looking as if
bombed

## The Void

Vast universe that you are,
I strain to comprehend you.

Where stars meet God
is a holy space of mystery.

Answers teeter on an edge,
a precipice unknown.

Black holes swallow light
and galaxies disappear.

Yet no babies are burped up,
nor flowers or thorns.

I fail to believe in this void
as source, as life force.

## The Station at Kharkiv

*On the Russian Invasion of Ukraine*

The train barely visible
The tracks going West unseen
A throng of people stretching
        to the reaches of vision
Jumbled and bundled together
Babies in parkas hoisted high
           Mamas' hands clasped tightly
Row after row after row
        Too steep to count
        Too deep to comprehend
Desperation an unheard shout
Danger a lurking shadow
Fear clearly visible

# Empty City

*On the Global Pandemic*

The people have all gone inside;
the sounds of the city have died
and a soft silence like snow has fallen
all over the street lamps and crossings
and benches where talking has ceased.

The co-mingling is missed, the scurry
of hurrying people and the lost tempo
of traffic—the rhythms of urban life.
A dullness descends, unspoken grief
at a place, still and mute, that once cried

out for our notice, for caution in face
of a stealthy foe, an illness creeping
on a cat's sly paws down our sidewalks
and up stairways and even across
lawns at our city's outer-most edge.

Paying little heed, we now pay a price
for our complacency, our nod of heads
at notions of sneaking death, as if we
could little comprehend the need
to rouse ourselves from quiet stupor.

So now the emptiness prevails, and
wails are all that can be heard, and sighs
that waft down among the shadows
from balconies and rooftops of a city
that has gathered itself inside, alone.

## Taken Away
*On the Global Pandemic*

Things that I love were taken away:
hugs from my grandkids, kisses galore,
trips to the store upon a whim
or an ache for fresh air and space.
Shared coffees with colleagues;
sundown cruises on a blue pontoon,
nestling side by side in the day's waning
rays. Peace of mind. Anticipatory joys.

Yet I feel no anguish at the loss
of a loved one, and I'm not bidding
good-bye on a cold, remote screen.
I have blessings: the sun still warms
my cheeks, the path through the nearby
woods offers red and gold leaves
for my feet to crunch. I can summon
hope; I can still envision tomorrow.

## Time's Up
*On the "Me, Too" Movement*

Can't you see how weary she is of fear?
Of packing mace and parking under lights
and peering backward at the fall of footsteps?

She is tired. Of being an object, a thing.
Of her body being eyeballed, her stride
eliciting whistles from passing he-wolves.

She reads reports of nearby rapes with dread
and debates signing up for beginning self-defense.
She alternates fear with fury. She stifles rage.

She has been stalked. She has been mocked.
She has been judged for her hair, her breasts,
her skin, her way to walk and sit and speak.

She is tired. She has a father, brothers, male
cousins and friends. She doesn't choose to hate
but she hates how men have shaped her life.

She yearns to be free—not of males but of men
who prey, who put down, who invalidate
her life as they pursue an unsavory lust.

She wonders. Who breeds these monsters
who pass for men? Who should she blame?
She ponders when she struggles to sleep.

In her dreams, she is always cornered. She
is the panicked quarry, with nowhere to hide.
She wakes, sweat drenched, eyes wild.

Enough, she thinks. Time's Up's the cry.
Me, too, she nods. I'm game to try to end
the chase and brave the fight and in sweet peace,
                    survive.

## Mother Grim

I fear to leave my children here
to wade the rising waters.
I foresee boots and stilts as footwear
in lifetimes of flooded hopes.
They say northern lands like Canada
will offer needed refuge; imagine
what the geese will think when
hordes of damp Americans
descend upon their homes.

I dread to leave my children here
to flee the raging flames.
I squint and see the Western skies
ablaze in reds and orange.
As heat beams scorch and sun
beats down, where will my children
run? With forests in ash and seas
all awash, they might seek crags
and peaks and high mounts above.

I ache to leave my children here
to face relentless scourge. As
illness spreads and new threats
emerge, who knows the throes
of disease they may continually
confront? If medicines run out
and suffering runs wild, I would
hate for any innocent child
to live in this hapless world.

I hate to leave my children here.

## Early Blue Violet

Weed, wildflower, vegetable—
the early blue violet being all three
fascinates me with its virtuosity.

Prolific along my hiking path,
early blue violets lend pops of color
to the otherwise brown-toned dolor

of grass that's slowly awakening.
Edible, but I doubt that I'd ever eat
their soft petals, despite how sweet

they're promised to be. I'd rather
pluck them to tuck in my hair
or float them in small bowl ware

to enjoy their heart-shaped faces.
I'd also gladly use them as pillows
when looking up as clouds billow

across the skies above the meadow.
As Spring arrives and winter ends,
I watch for them, nature's gems.

## Dead End

A fishy, foul smell rose from the rocks below
and a few eye-balling carcasses lay splayed flat
where the water lapped up against the pilings.

Two grizzled guys loitered by the cars parked
in the five or six spaces allotted for the public.
An unmistakable Brooklyn accent cut the quiet.

I squinted, trying to shut out the tawdry scene
and focus on the crystalline blue water, the sails—
an impressionistic painting spread across my mind.

Behind me, the yellow canopies of a yacht club
rippled in the soft June breeze while tinkling sounds
of glassware and conversation wafted on the air.

This spot was the Dead End marked on the sign
that signaled outsiders to turn back, conveyed
notice that this was private, privileged ground

except for the small, squat parking lot reserved
for the lucky few who drove in early enough
to secure the cheap seats for a view of the bay.

And so the glimmering sea held my gaze, sure
as I was that Greenwich's cozy access should
not be denied me, a mere traveler on my way.

## The Willow

A weeping willow leans
far over the lapping waters
of the lake and creates
a little sylvan cave
where I meditate.

Rustling leaves look
silvery as the summer air
tussles them and strands
of my hair in this place
where I contemplate.

I could read here
in this secluded haven
or bask in slant rays
of sun but my willow
is instead where I pray.

## Storm Over the Gulf

The air is sticky and damp as a heaviness
hovers, making it hard to breathe. The sky
wears a yellowish tint, but in the distance
is dark with a purplish hue. Leaves
on the trees fold under, protecting limbs
and branches from the oncoming onslaught.
The air is still and even birds are quiet;
all of nature hesitates, waiting.

A slight breeze stirs first as sand skitters
along the water's edge. Waves rush in,
cresting with a thicker foam;
sea water turns more deep green
than blue. Sea gulls circle overhead,
unsure whether to fly or land. Awnings
and table umbrellas flap wildly
in the gathering wind. Temperatures drop.

Sunbathers and swimmers empty
the beach; even the pilings appear
to shift in the suds created by frothing
water. An ominous rumbling sweeps
in across the waves, and the sky descends
into the sea. Coming at a furious slant,
rain begins to pelt the landscape. Within
minutes, another Gulf storm has arrived.

## Hondo, New Mexico

Hondo has packed up and left.
Scrub grass, dry leaves, heat remain.
A dilapidated frame building leans
toward the dusty road as we slow
to peer: U.S. Post Office. A sepia
wash colors the setting with soft
tones of brown and stucco reds.

Vivid doesn't thrive in Hondo.
Yet the southwestern sun still
glitters against the faded scene.
Tumbleweed skitters past us,
the only motion besides the sweep
of wind, muted sighs—sounds
of ghosts who once awaited mail.

## October on the Shore

I find a gray-dead log of driftwood and sit,
content to turn my face toward brisk wind

and strain to catch the last feeble rays
of summer on my nose and cheeks and hair.

Iridescent blues of water in June and July
have darkened into shades of navy and slate,

and as waves crest and crash against the shore,
they converse with me in less rapturous tones.

Even the seagulls seem less intent on making
friends, and the sandpipers have lost their skip.

There is a stark beauty, however, to the shore
in Fall, and I feel a greedy pleasure in not having

to share. When I rise and climb among the rocks,
bracing air lifts my spirits despite the time

of parting. I find invigoration in solitude,
the panoramic landscape, even grit of cold sand

between my bare toes. I feel inspired, despite
the waning year, despite a weakening sun,

despite the desolation of winter sure to come.
It's me and the shore together, alive, communing

one last time before icy winds blow, waves
sculpt in place, and I am forced to retreat alone.

## Bigger Than Life

You were bigger than life
Known by everyone in our northern town
Accepted fresh mushrooms and walleye
    for legal fees from locals
Attended viewings at the funeral home
    for friends and clients without fail

You played a mean hand of gin rummy
Quit smoking over and over and over again
Took drives on country roads just
    to take the wheel
Knew every precinct and precinct
    committeeman on a first-name basis

When I had to ask you to leave because
    you kicked the dog
your eyes traveled a distance far away
    and clouded over with pain
You left without a word but the
    silence spoke estrangement

When you passed, the line of mourners
    stretched out the door and down the block
One older man who shook my hand
    said proudly *He was my attorney*
Although an enigma to me in many ways
    I answered proudly *He was my father*

## Place of Peace

Elisabeth sleeps,
knees curled against my groin,
my knees tucked around her toes,
my mother body
encircling her daughter body—
warming the nest,
lining the nest—nesting.

Our cheeks pressed,
her breaths puff evenly,
play a soft cadence
against my skin.
The space between us
is moist and close,
and a flutter
of her tiny lashes
touches, tickles lightly.

Nestled as we are,
her slumber becoming
my poetry,
I commit the feel
of this little one's life song
to memory—
that I might at any moment
recreate this place of peace.

**Critters**

We nursed two baby gators, shipped home
from a family trip to Florida in the '50s
by our mother, who shopped for novelty
and respite from boredom. Naming the boxed
creatures Caesar and Cicero, she fed them
raw burger over the kitchen sink, poking bits
down pink throats with a baby spoon.

She giggled while I, aged eight, grimaced
and gagged. Three turtles gurgled nearby
in a tiny terrarium, bedecked with dark rocks
and blades of grass and a "pond" that turned
to slime. Their smell still haunts my memory,
an odor only turtles can emit. When one
crawled over the edge and under a bed, I
staged a mutiny, refusing to sleep in that room
until the stinky, crawly thing was caught.

Meanwhile, the gators, not desiring to live
out their lives in a plastic tub on a linoleum
floor, soon perished. What our mother thought
would become of them—or us—once they
grew in size remains a question of inestimable
curiosity. Upon their demise, my mother
may have mourned their loss, but my sister
and I needed little to no consolation.

## Touring

More than the rules of the game,
I remember the setting: the blonde
dining table, the street light shining
through the sheer curtains, the jade
ash tray collecting dirty cigar stubs.
Coke bottles littering the four corners,
popcorn kernels strewn in a haphazard
way. Dad seated at the head of the table,
presiding. An old sea dog, *Captain
of the Pacific Fleet.* He who had dealt
many rounds of cards in the bowels
of the *New Mexico* battleship must
have found our family coterie quite tame.
Yet we were delighted to have his
attention, a rare thing. There he sat,
Cutty Sark at his elbow, *El Camino*
crunched in the corner of his mouth,
angling for another gasoline card—
the card that kept you on the road.
That was the aim of the game, I
remember—to keep the engine going,
to keep touring the country, back when
WWII guys like Dad thought a drive
on an open road equaled the freedom
for which they had risked their lives.

## Carbonation and Salt

Hearing my daughter retch
as if something wild is catching
at her throat and choking her
causes me to press my forehead
against the closed bathroom door
and offer ginger ale and saltines
and my ricocheting blood pressure
as penance for her suffering.

Searching in my mind for images
of my own first effort at birthing,
I recall waves of queasiness—
soothed only by blue popsicles
and bland mashed potatoes
and afternoon naps—that eased
in evenings and dark of night.

But I don't recall Friday evenings
spent sprawled beside toilet bowls,
my eyes bleary with fatigue
and my cheeks pale as chalk
and my fingers clenched tight
like hers as she fights to be brave
in this all-new venture of
bringing life into the world.

Mother of the mother-to-be, I
feel immersed in her misery, just
as I hope to be bonded in her joy.
But this first trimester is long,
and the trials are tough, and I
can do little more than lean
against the door and offer small
comforts—carbonation and salt.

# A Clear Wriggler
*For Bronson*

Found in the South Pacific, this skinny fish
also swims the waters of the Western Pacific.
My grandson recognizes this fish, because,
as he puts it, *I know my fish.* He is only three,
but his little mind is a species catalogue,
and *Xenisthmus clarus* is captured there.

Bronson can explain about the disappearance
of the dinosaurs, noting solemnly that all
of us—he, his little brother, his mommy and
daddy—all of us will "die out" someday,
just like the pre-historics did. (His mommy dabs
her eyes; I gulp some air.)

The little tyke also loves woodland sprites
and animals of the rain forest. Yet his mind
races ahead: *We will all be together
with God,* he says. (How does he know
about God?) He observes birds and bugs
and small critters that scamper among trees
near his home. But fish are his favorites—
even the prehistoric fish called dinosaurs.

He knows more than he can possibly
understand. With a memory like a
clam trap, he retains facts far beyond
his years. He knows about the chosen
waters of the Clear Wiggler, but he
has no concept of vast oceans or geographic
clime. He can identify thirty dinosaurs,
but he has no real way to measure time.

Yet he is the one who seems to know
where we're going—the way of the
dinosaur, the Clear Wiggler, and all
those we love. His three-year-old mind
far outstretches mine.

29

## Forever Like This
*For Tatum*

Our breathing rises and falls in tandem,
his moist blonde curls wet against my chest,
his sweet plump cheeks pressed against my neck,
his pudgy warm hands splayed across my shoulders.

> *I could live forever like this, in this embrace,*
> *in this same space in a creaking old rocker*
> *in a sun-splashed room with this baby held close.*

Whatever God deigned peace to be, it is this place
in time for me, this simple act of rocking, rocking
a precious child whose fluttery soft breaths
pulse with the essence of innocence, pure love.

The pangs I feel go deep and full, deep into a heart
that has known babies before, has known this peace
before, but knows this may be the last to be
mine, as mother or from mother's child, the last in line.

As our breathing rises and falls in tandem, tears
also fall, trickling silently down my face onto baby's
golden locks, glinting as they land, not awakening
but anointing him as only a grandmother's love can.

**Marjie Giffin** is a Midwestern writer who resides in Indianapolis, where she serves as a Poetry Reader for the Indiana Writers Center's literary journal, *Flying Island*. She was educated at Indiana University in Bloomington, Indiana, and earned an M.A. degree in English from Butler University in Indianapolis. She also earned certification in gifted/talented education from Indiana University-Purdue University Indianapolis and has taught both college-level writing and middle school gifted education.

Early in her career, Marjie authored four regional histories: *Water Runs Downhill, If Tables Could Talk, A Walk Through Time,* and an abbreviated history for the Newcomen Association. She also wrote *A Middle School Guide to Literary Terms* with co-author Mary Ann Yedinak.

Marjie's poetry has appeared in *Synkroniciti, Blue Heron Review, Flying Island, Tipton Poetry Journal, Saint Katherine Review, Agape Review, Of Rust and Glass, Poetry Quarterly, Northwest Indiana Literary Journal, Snapdragon: A Journal of Healing and Art,* and was featured in an issue of the *Heartland Society of Women Writers.* Additional poems have been published in *So It Goes: The Kurt Vonnegut Literary Journal* and the anthologies *The World We Live(d) In: An Anthology of Poems About Social Justice; What Was and Will Be: Life in the Time of COVID-19; Reflections on Little Creek; Leave Them Something;* and *Stormwash: Environmental Poems.*

Marjie's first chapbook, *Touring,* was published by Finishing Line Press in 2021, and three of her poems were selected for the Indiana Poetry Archive, *INverse,* in 2023.

Marjie's free time is spent with her family of three adult children and six active grandchildren and, until he passed away in late 2023, her husband Ken Giffin. She also enjoys reading, travel, current events, and time spent with friends, including the four other members of her local poetry workshop.

www.ingramcontent.com/pod-product-compliance
Lightning Source LLC
Chambersburg PA
CBHW022054080426
42734CB00009B/1336